Günter Gerngross • Herbert Puchta

PLAYWAY 2

TO

ENGLISH

Picture Cards

for vocabulary presentation and practice

Illustrations by Svjetlan Junaković

ISBN 0521 656818

Layout by Gio Festin

© Cambridge University Press and Helbling, Rum/Innsbruck 1998

Helbling

CAMBRIDGE
UNIVERSITY PRESS

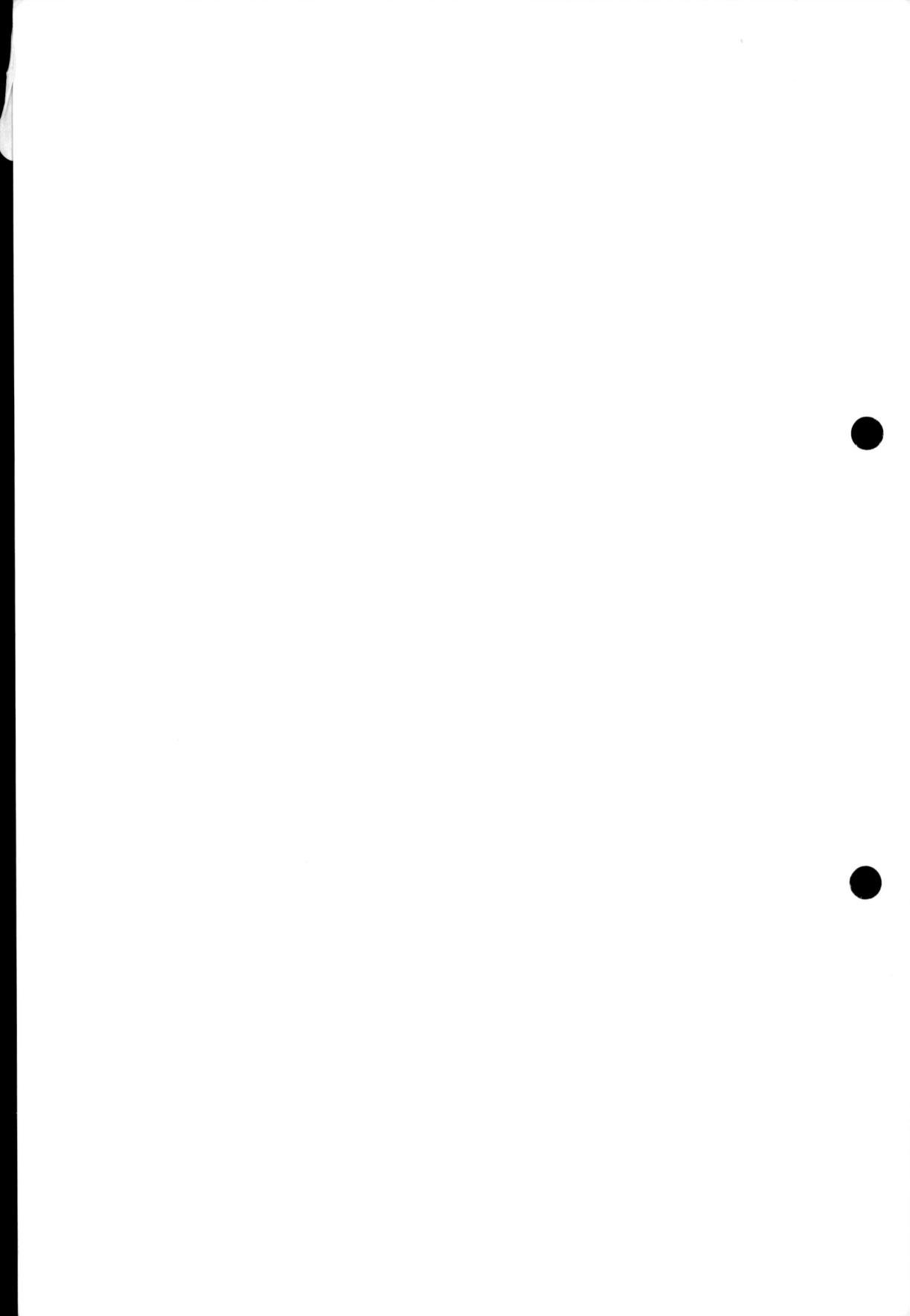

CONTENTS

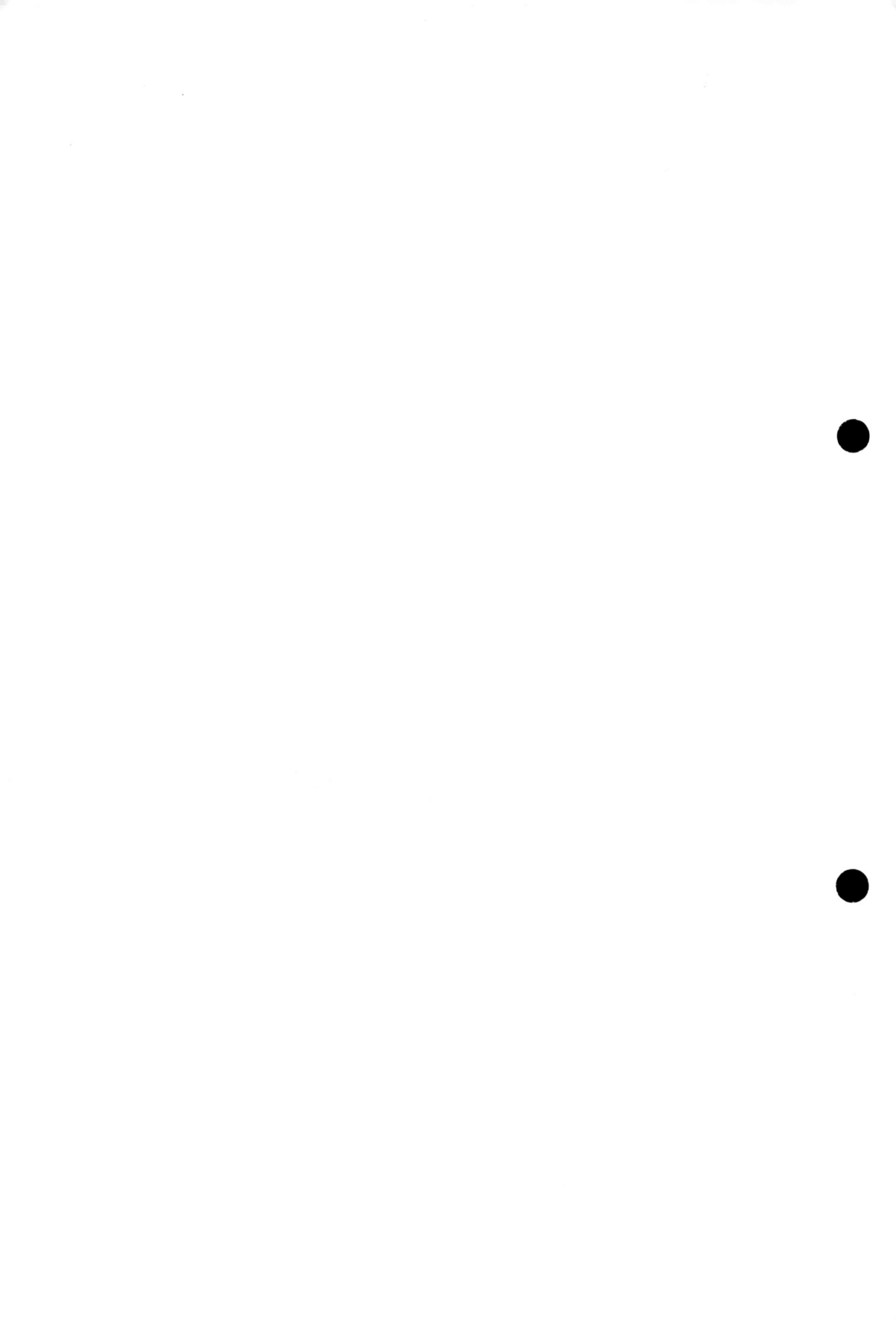

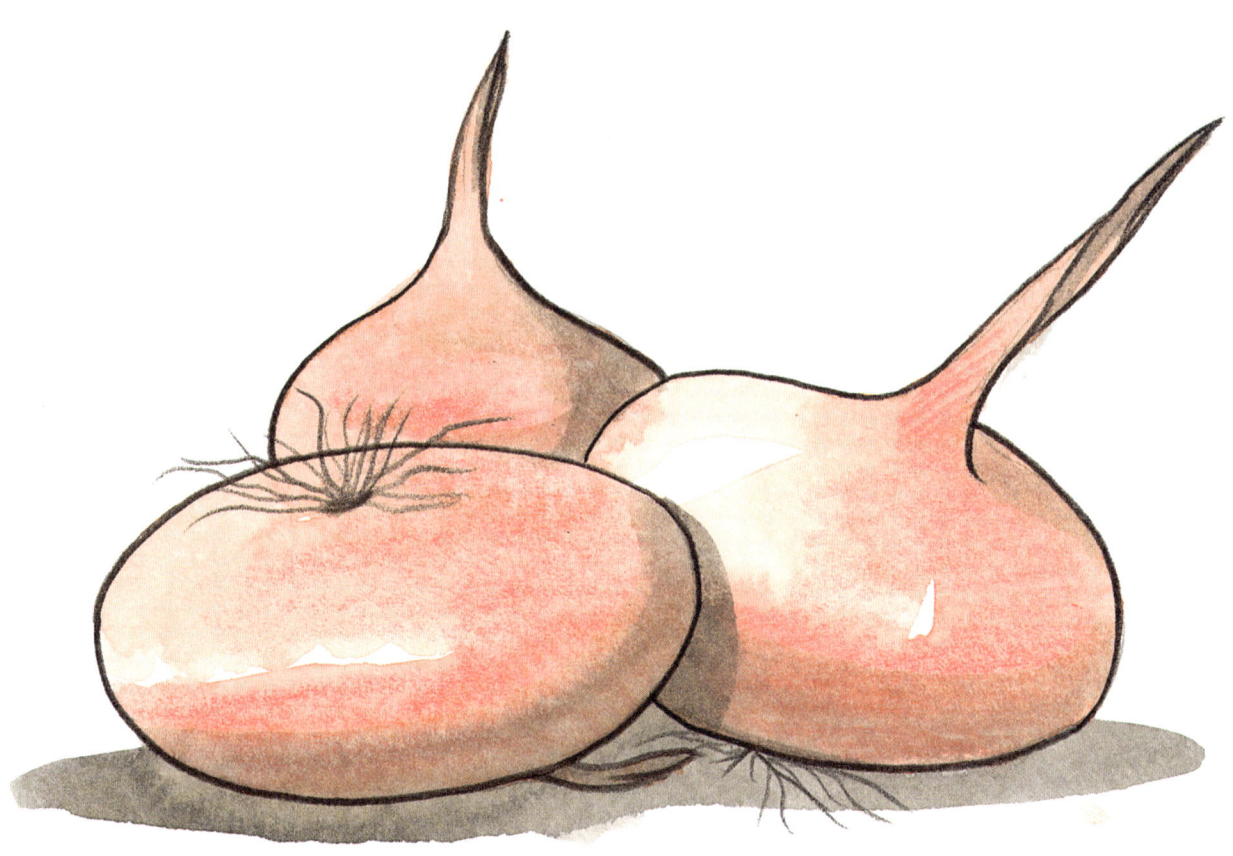

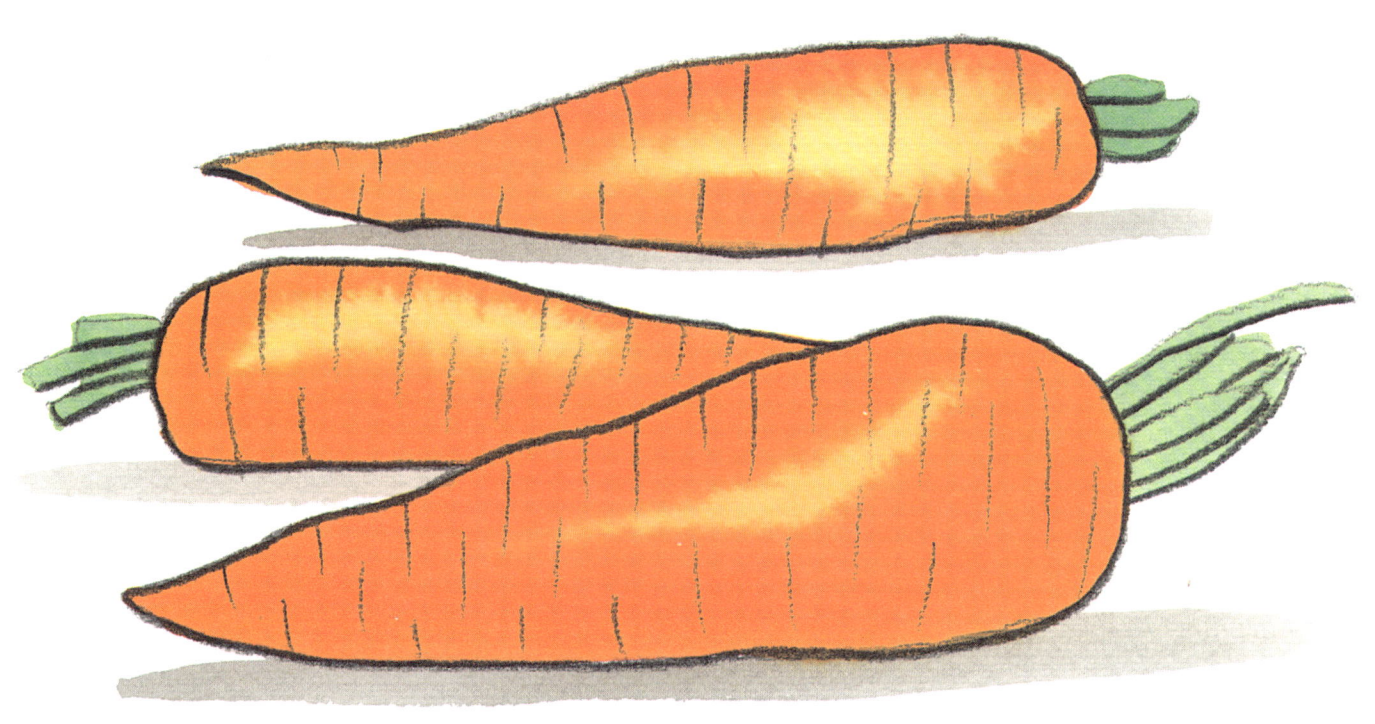

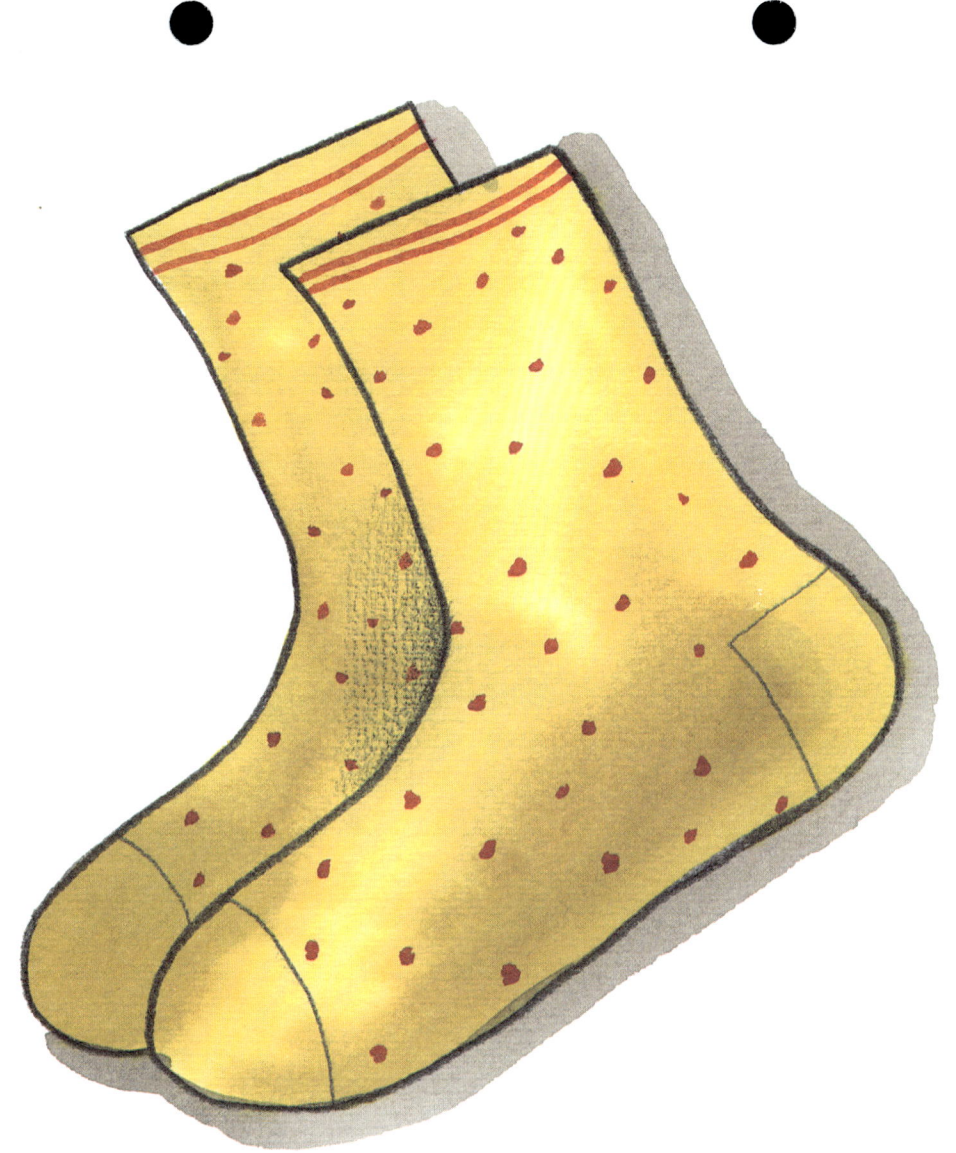

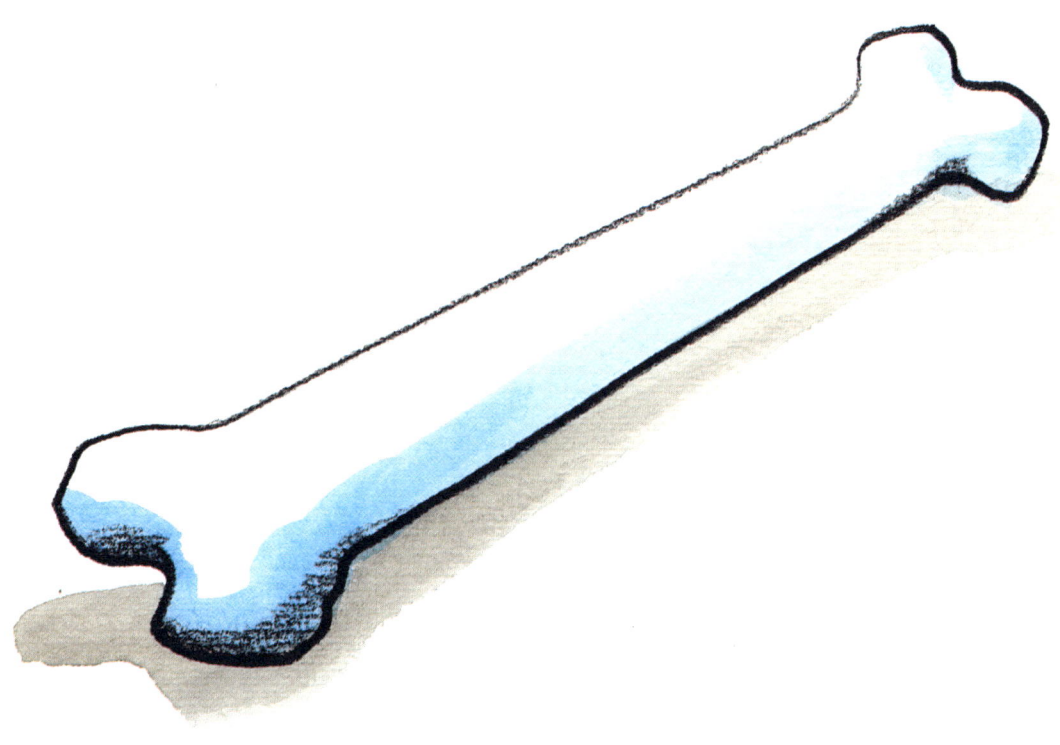

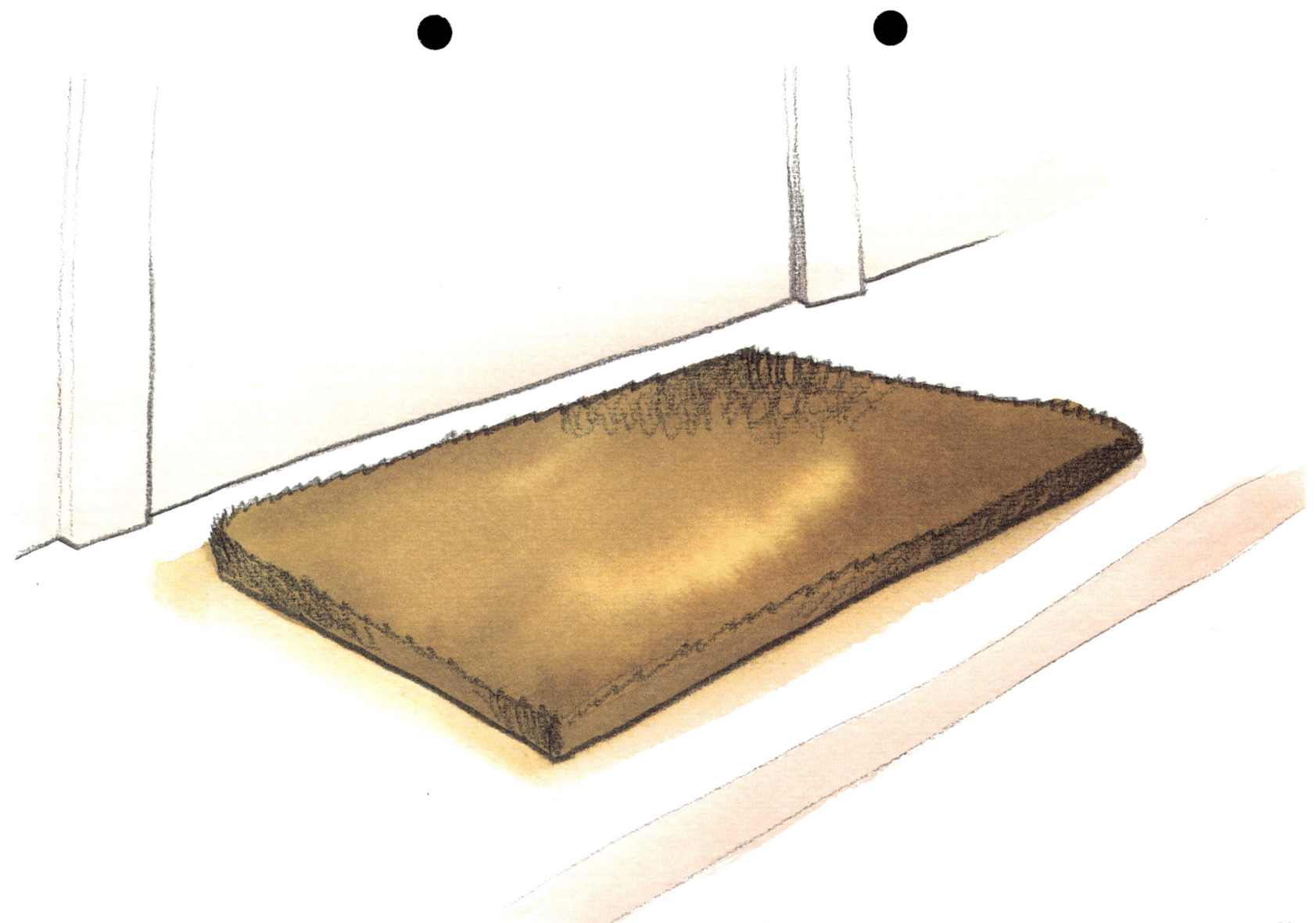

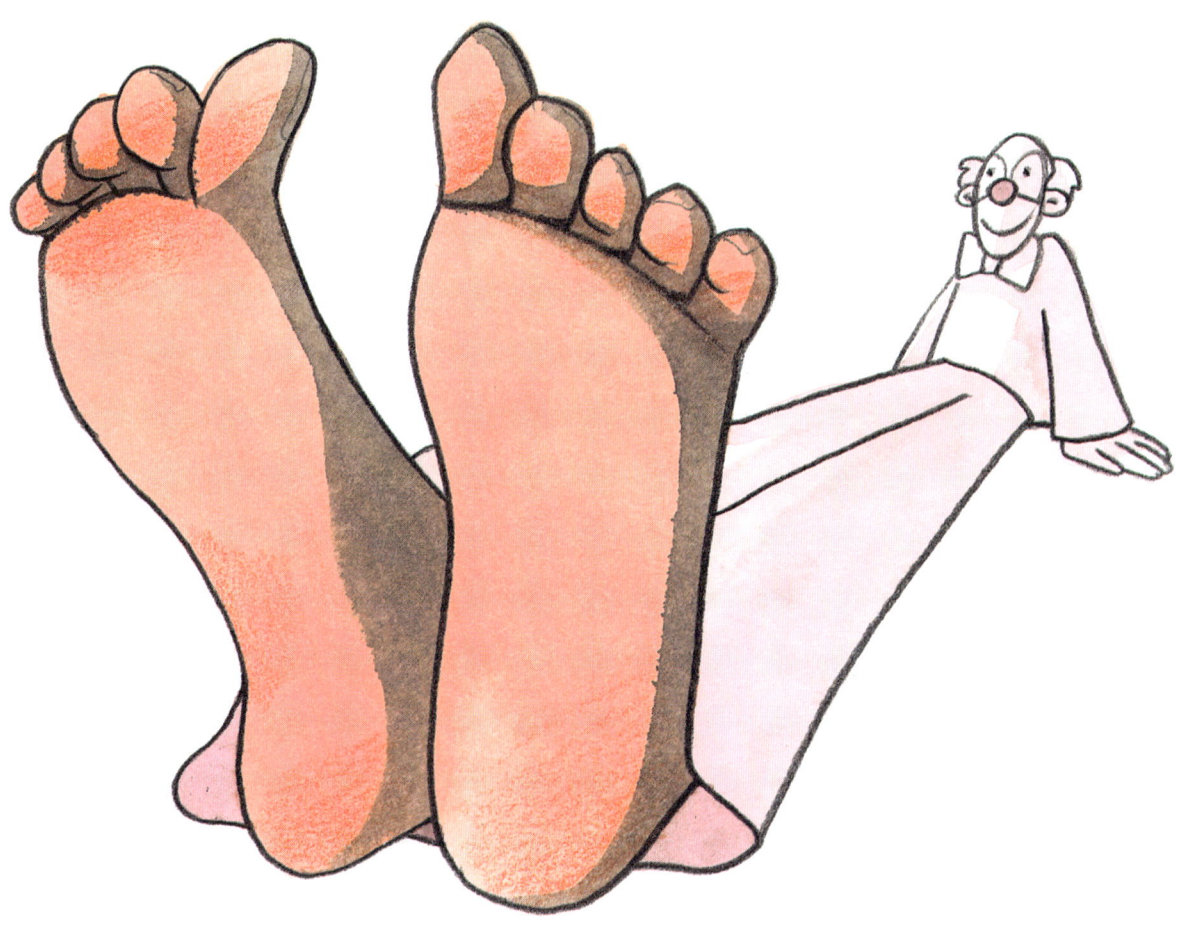

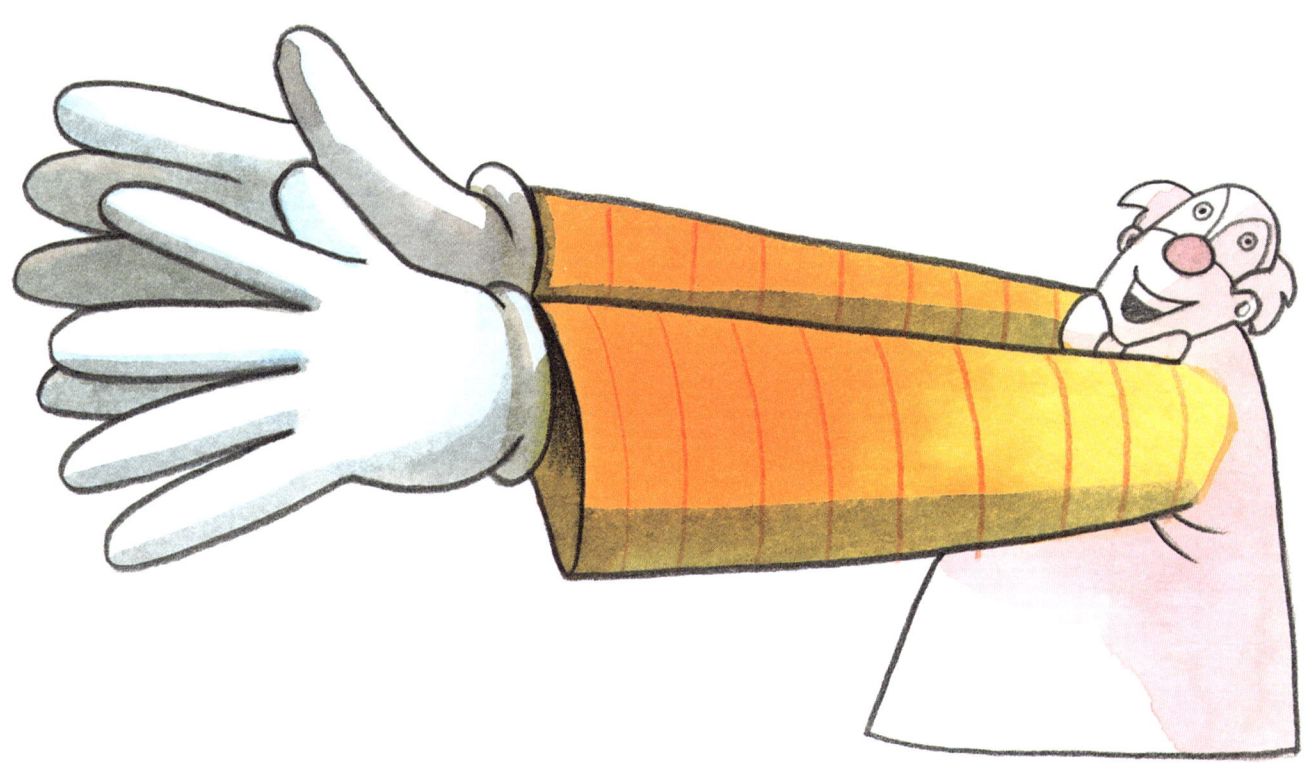

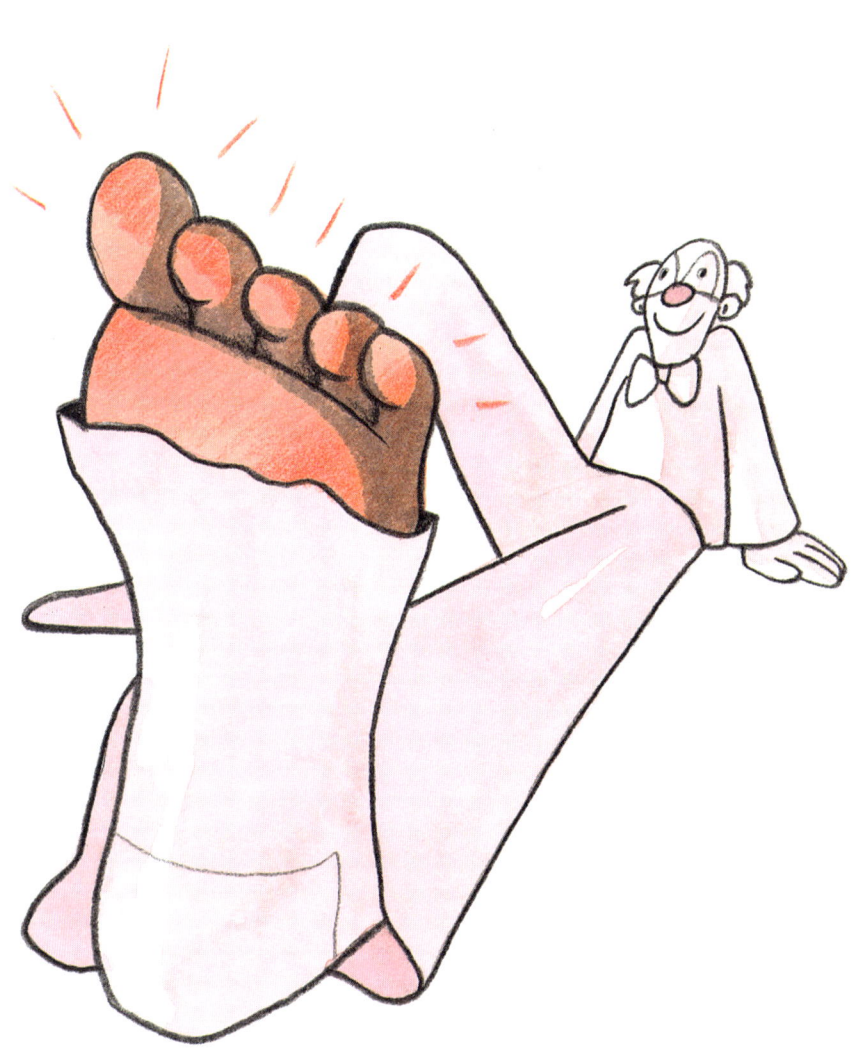

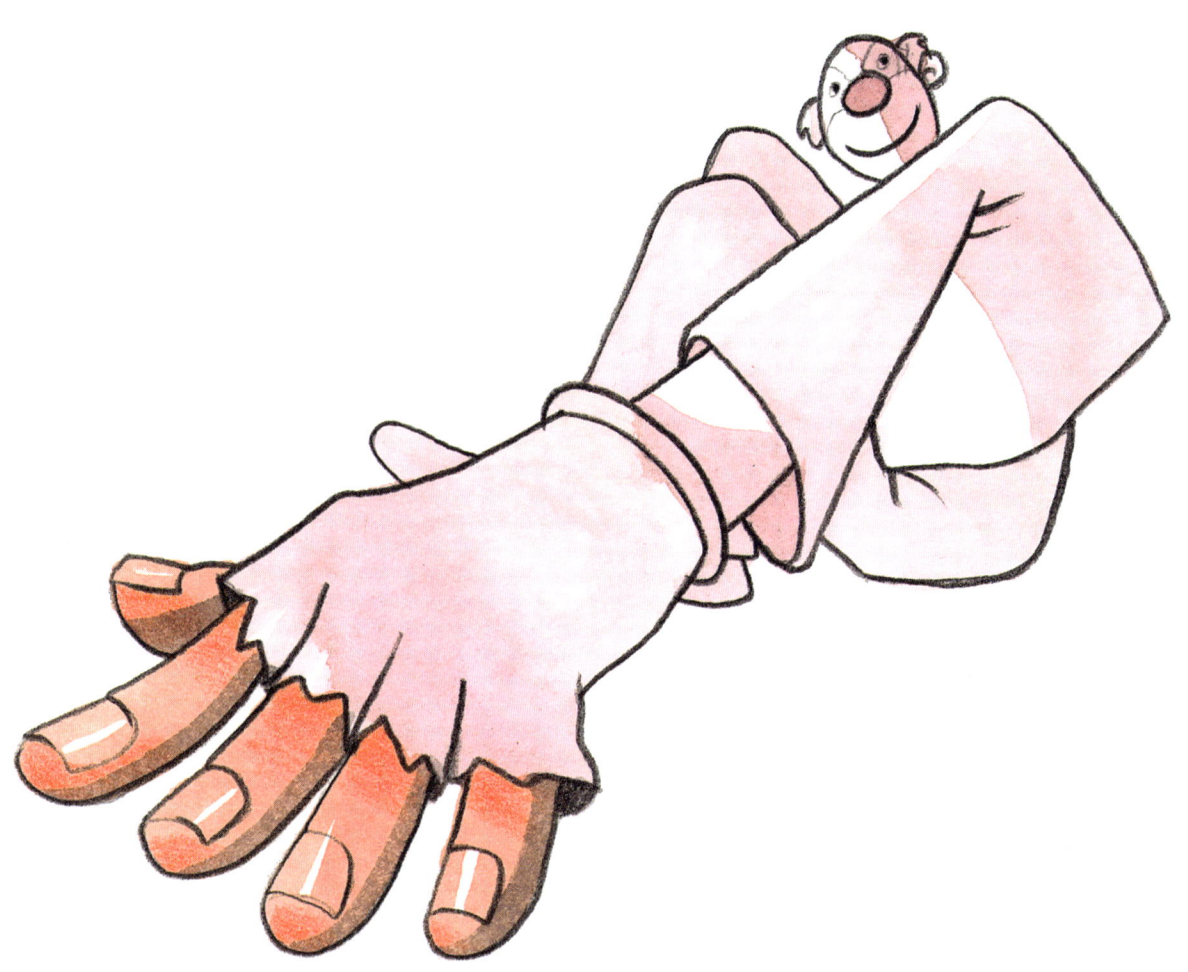

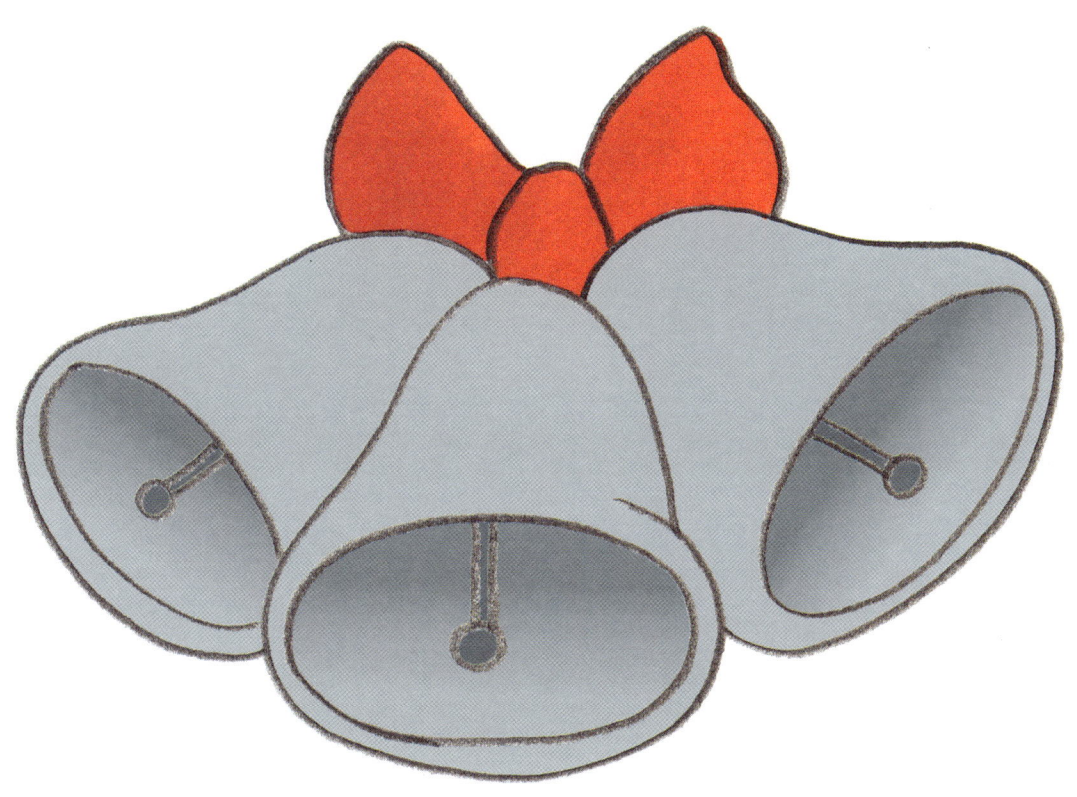